PRESENTED BY

Elizabeth Eastham

1986

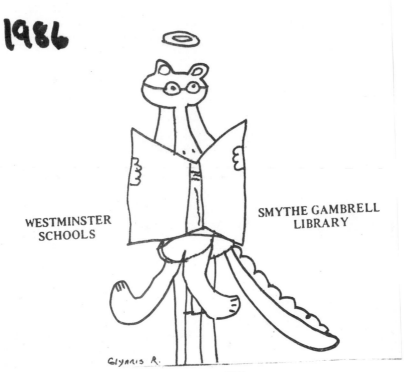

WESTMINSTER
SCHOOLS

SMYTHE GAMBRELL
LIBRARY

Glynnis R.

A New True Book

PRAIRIES AND GRASSLANDS

Written and photographed
By James P. Rowan

This "true book" was prepared
under the direction of
Illa Podendorf,
formerly with the Laboratory School,
University of Chicago

CHILDRENS PRESS, CHICAGO

Prickly poppy

Dedicated to Dr. Robert F. Betz

Cover— Fort Phil Kearny historical site, Story, Wyoming

Library of Congress Cataloging in Publication Data

Rowan, James P.
  Prairies and grasslands.

  (A New true book)
  Includes index.
  Summary: Discusses the plant and animal life of
prairies and grasslands throughout the world.
  1. Prairie ecology—Juvenile literature. 2. Grassland ecology—Juvenile literature. [1. Prairie ecology
2. Grassland ecology. 3. Ecology] I. Title.
QH541.5.P7R63 1983   574.5'2643   83-7310
ISBN 0-516-01706-3   AACR2

TABLE OF CONTENTS

Cream false indigo

4

WHAT IS A PRAIRIE?

A prairie is a place made up of plants and animals that can live only under special conditions. A prairie will grow only when it gets just the right amount of rain. If there is too much rain, a forest will grow. If there is too little rain, a desert will grow.

Dr. Robert Betz burning a prairie

Fires are important
for the growth of a
prairie. Fires are bad
when they burn in a
forest. But fires are good
for a prairie. They burn

away trees and shrubs that have moved into the prairie from the surrounding forest. If these were not burned away every few years, the prairie would in time disappear. The fire also turns old, dead plants into ash. This ash fertilizes the soil for new growth.

Above: Blazing star
Above right: Tickseed sunflower
Right: Purple coneflower
Below right: Green milkweed
Below: Fringed gentian

Prairies are sometimes called grasslands. Do you know why? Grass is the most common plant growing there. But growing among the different kinds of grasses are many other plants. Sunflowers, coneflowers, gentians, milkweeds, and blazing stars are some of the prairies' wild flowers.

Some people call any large, open field or space a prairie, but many of these are only fields of weeds. If you cleared the field and let it alone for a few months, the weeds would grow back. Very few real prairie plants would grow in an area like that. In fact, some prairie plants can grow only where the land has not been disturbed for many years.

Blue Mounds State Park, Minnesota

PRAIRIES
OF THE WORLD

Prairies are found all over the world. In North America, prairies are found from the Midwest to the Rocky Mountains. In Africa, prairies are found in the

Tsavo West National Park, Kenya

African elephants on Masai Mara National Reserve

eastern part of that continent from Kenya to South Africa. Here the prairie is called the *veldt*. When there are scattered trees on the prairie, it is called a *savanna*.

South America has prairies that are called *pampas*. In Eurasia, the prairies are called *steppes*. There are even prairies in Australia.

ANIMALS OF THE PRAIRIE

Many different kinds of animals live on prairies. Like the prairie plants, many of these animals cannot live anywhere else. Bison, pronghorn, elk, and prairie dogs are a few of the animals that live on North American prairies. Prairie dogs live in large groups called towns. They clear the

Black-tailed prairie dog

grass away from their
burrows so they can
watch for enemies.

There were once so
many bison in North
America that it
sometimes took days for
a single herd to pass.
Most of the bison are
gone now. But bison still
live in some national
parks.

Bison at Osborne Conservation Center in Iowa

Pronghorn are like antelope. They have large eyes to watch for enemies. Pronghorn are the fastest runners on the American prairie.

Left: Pronghorn
Below: North American elk

18

Above: Warthog
Left: Giraffe

On the grasslands of
East Africa many animals
live together. Giraffes,
zebras, warthogs,
antelope, ostriches, and
buffalo all make their
home there. Many of
these plant-eating
animals are fast runners.

Above: Zebras
Middle right: Ostrich with young
Far right: Thomson's gazelle

They have to be fast because there are few trees and shrubs where they can hide from their enemies. The meat-eating animals in these grasslands have to be very fast, too.

Above: African lion (male)
Left: Cheetah

The cheetah is a cat that eats small antelope. It has very long legs and is the fastest animal in the world. Lions live there, too. They live and hunt together in family groups called prides.

South American rhea

The South American pampas have many animals, too. The rhea is a large bird. It looks something like an ostrich. It can run at great speeds across the grassland on its large legs. Its wings are so small it cannot fly.

Above: Giant anteater from South America
Left: Termite mound on Australian grassland

The giant anteater has
no teeth, but has very
large claws on its front
legs. With these, it rips
open ant and termite
nests. It licks up the
insects with its long
sticky tongue.

Above: Wisents from Eurasia
Left: Giant armadillo from South America

Another animal from the pampas with big claws is the giant armadillo. Its large front claws are used to dig burrows where it lives during the day.

The wisent and Przewalski's horse are two animals that come from the Eurasian steppes.

Above: Przewalski's horse from Eurasia
Left: Kangaroos from Australia

They are both rare. They are being saved from extinction in zoos around the world.

Many kinds of kangaroos live on the Australian plains.

25

Above: Bumblebee
Above left: Monarch butterfly on blazing star
Right: Indian paintbrush

INSECTS AND SPIDERS

When people talk about prairie animals, they do not usually think of insects and spiders. There are many thousands of kinds of these animals. They are important members of the prairie community. Many wild flowers are pollinated by the prairie's bees, flies, butterflies,

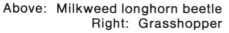

Above: Milkweed longhorn beetle
Right: Grasshopper

and moths. Beetles, bugs, wasps, and grasshoppers live on the prairie, too.

On a prairie only a few kinds of spiders build webs. This is because there is nothing to save the webs from being torn apart by strong winds. Also, few prairie plants are strong enough to support webs. Some spiders look like the flowers they hide in where they wait for

Crab spider

Wolf spider

Jumping spider

insects to eat. Other spiders, such as wolf spiders, live on the ground and chase their prey. The jumping spiders have large eyes and live among the leaves of prairie plants. Here they hunt for small insects, stalking them like a cat and finally leaping onto them.

PEOPLE AND THE PRAIRIE

People have always
lived on or near prairies.
In fact, the first manlike
creatures in the world
probably lived in the
grasslands and
savannas of East Africa.

Masai
people in
Kenya

Today in East Africa,
some tribes still live in
these same grasslands.
The Masai people of

Masai cattle

Children of the Masai in Kenya

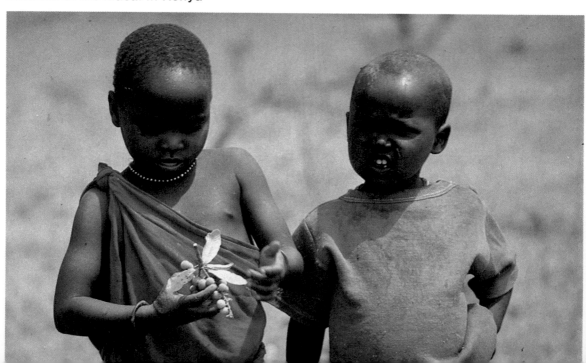

Kenya and Tanzania
raise cattle and graze
them on the grass near
giraffes and zebras. They
bring them inside a
strong corral of
thornbush at night to
protect them from lions
and leopards.

Plains Indian hunting bison

Mandan earth lodge

In North America, many Indian tribes lived on the prairie. Some tribes followed the bison herds from place to place. They moved their villages to where these animals were. Some tribes lived in one place for a long time and farmed the land. They made homes out of earth and logs.

Today, many prairies are disappearing. People have found many uses for them. Some are destroyed because the soil underneath the prairie is good for farming. Some of the best farming in the world is in the Midwest of North America. Some

Illinois farmland

Wisconsin farmland

states such as Illinois and Iowa were once almost all prairie. Today only a few small areas of prairie remain.

Cattle grazing also destroys prairies. Many prairie plants cannot live when they are always being chewed and walked on by cattle. The sharp hooves of cattle

Cattle

can dig up the soil and
kill the plants. When this
happens, the land is
taken over by weeds, or
it can even turn into a
desert.

SAVING PRAIRIES

Prairies are beautiful
places, and many people
are working to save
them. National parks and
wildlife sanctuaries have

been created so that some prairies will never be turned into farms. Some of them are burned by scientists so that the grass will grow better the following year. Here the animals are protected from hunters and poachers. They are allowed to live out their lives without fear of humans.

Markham prairie

Let us hope there will always be prairies and grasslands in the world for us to enjoy. It is up to us to make sure that the many kinds of plants and animals making their homes there will always have a place to live.

WORDS YOU SHOULD KNOW

antelope(AN •tuh •loap)—a mammal that has horns

armadillo(ar •ma •DILL •oh)—a mammal that burrows and who has a bony covering that looks like armor

bison(BY •sun)—a large mammal of western North America with a shaggy dark-brown mane and short, curved horns; buffalo

burrow(BER •oh)—to dig a hole or tunnel under the ground

cheetah(CHEE •tah)—a spotted wild cat of Africa and southern Asia that has long legs and can run very fast

continent(KAHN •tin •ent)—one of the seven large landmasses of the earth

corral(kor •RAL)—an enclosed pen or a place for keeping cattle and other animals

create(kree •AIT)—to make or produce

destroy(des •TROY)—wipe out; ruin

disturb(diss •TERB)—upset; to change

elk—a large deer with antlers that lives in North America

extinct(ex •TINKT)—no longer in existence

fertilize(FER •til •ize)—to put a substance on plants or soil so things will grow faster and better

Masai(mah •SYE)—a group of people of East Africa

pampas(PAM •pahss)—large grasslands in South America

plain(PLAYN)—a large, flat area of land without any trees

poach(POH •ch)—to hunt or fish in places where it is not allowed

pollinate(POL •in •ate)—to transfer pollen to the female part of a flower

prey(PRAY)—to hunt or capture other animals

pride(PRYDE)—a group of lions that live together

pronghorn(PRONG •horn)—a type of antelope that has short, forked horns that lives in western North America

Przewalski horse(puhr •zheh •VAHL •skihz)—a small horse that lives on Eurasian prairie

rare(RAIR)—not found or seen very often

rhea(REE • ah)—a very large bird of South America

sanctuary(SANK • chu • airy)—an area where animals live and are protected

savanna(suh • VAN • uh)—a large, flat plain with scattered trees

stalk(STAWK)—to follow in a quiet, careful way so you are not noticed

steppe(STEP)—a Eurasian prairie

surround(sir • ROUND)—to be on all sides; to enclose

thornbush(THORN • bush)—a small, low plant that has sharp points on the stem

veldt(VELD)—a large, flat open country covered with grass in South Africa

warthog(WORT • hog)—a wild hog found in Africa

wisent(WYE • zent)—a mammal that lives on the Eurasian steppe

INDEX

About the Author

James P. Rowan majored in zoology and geology at Northeastern Illinois University. He is currently a keeper in the reptile house at Lincoln Park Zoo in Chicago, Illinois. A professional photographer, Jim and his wife Jan have traveled around the world photographing animals, insects, and nature. He has more than forty thousand images on file and is adding hundreds of new subjects to his collection each year. His photographs have been published in a number of encyclopedias, textbooks, and magazines.